The Flea, the Minnow, the Elephant, and the Whale

The Flea, the Minnow, the Elephant, and the Whale

Parables for the Twenty-first Century

Glenn Goree

RESOURCE *Publications* • Eugene, Oregon

THE FLEA, THE MINNOW, THE ELEPHANT, AND THE WHALE
Parables for the Twenty-first Century

Resource Publications
An Imprint of Wipf and Stock Publishers
199 W. 8th Ave., Suite 3
Eugene, OR 97401

www.wipfandstock.com

PAPERBACK ISBN: 978-1-5326-0232-0
HARDCOVER ISBN: 978-1-5326-0234-4
EBOOK ISBN: 978-1-5326-0233-7

Manufactured in the U.S.A.

I dedicate this book to the five most important women in my life.

My wife, Valerie, my life and light.
My mother, Neva, my rock and foundation.
My daughter, Colleen, my wise, gentle, compassionate angel.
My daughter-in-law, Minerva, my quiet thoughtful muse.

And finally,

My granddaughter, Xaia, who is a blossoming rose
of femininity and womanhood,
and who has always had a sweet spirit.

Contents

Introduction: Why a Flea, a Minnow, an Elephant, and a Whale Decided to Talk

Who would guess the four of us would decide to talk?
But we banded together in private, to speak our piece where
no human could balk.

Great theologians have written on the topics within
these following pages,
But the average Christian has bills to pay, and jobs to do, so they
aren't theological sages.

Therefore, some of us in the animal kingdom decided to hold
a special conference.
We asked ourselves what we could do to help man improve his lot,
to make a difference.

Farm animals have always been in Biblical stories since Christ was born,
So it was a unanimous decision to select us four, since we're not the norm.

We decided to teach Biblical truths for humans to learn what's
most important in life,
Because they are from the four of us, routinely hunted with hook,
gun, and knife.

We thought parables would be entertaining and better remembered
without much mental strife.
So we pray you enjoy what our author has written
on our humble behalf.

Parable One: A Dream, Not a Scheme

There was once a tiny minnow who swam boldly,
He was scarcely a trifle long, mostly.

In fact, when he turned to face you,
He was not much wider than a folded tissue.

But he had a dream.

Deep inside he felt there was more to life than his salty aquatics,
All the fish in his dark world swam around blindly, robotic,
And they fell in line behind each other without question, hypnotic.

But he had a dream,

His fish brethren said he swam against their school.
They told him to fall in line or else he risked being a fool.
He needed their protection from man's hook, reel, and spool.
Besides, being different didn't make him cool.

But he had a dream.

He preached to his fellows, "You swim in blindness without question.
You follow one behind the other without hesitation.
But unlike you who are settled and content,
I want something more than what this dull life has sent."

And he had a dream.

Parable One: A Dream, Not a Scheme

Suddenly, a large net from above missed all the fish except one.
Yes, it was our hero, who in his brief life had finally won,
As he was hauled to the surface to feel the warm light of the sun.
He told all who watched in horror that his life was not over, but just begun.

He found his dream.

His last words heard before he left the deep's safety
Was an exhortation to all who had thought he was crazy.
"Sometimes to gain your life you must risk death.
To find what your heart says is right, to inhale a new breath."

He lived his dream.

The net hurled him high into the air,
And he saw a new world he dreamed had to be there.
But the net's hold on him was not square,
So it tossed him free beyond where no other fish would dare.

And as he re-entered the ocean's water,
He braved a new world order.

Parable Two: But by God's Grace

Said the flea to the elephant,
"Be gone! Your being is an affront!"

Said the minnow to the whale,
"Go around! I need room to inhale!"

Said the earth to planets near and far,
"Worship me! Man is master under the stars!"

The elephant stepped on the flea,
The whale swallowed the minnow instantly.

Then a voice from distances unknown,
Made all existence fearfully wail and moan,

"Who are you to tell me?
Did you form the dry land and sea?

In My grace you exist at all,
In only My mercy man can stand tall."

Parable Three: Security

A flea stood tall on an elephant's back.
"My world is secure. There's nothing I lack."

A minnow attached himself to a whale.
"I'll cling to him. He's safe in any gale."

A flood washed poor elephant away,
This of course did not make flea's day.

A great noise with fire and harpoon,
Left minnow with a bad afternoon.

A Mighty Voice from the Heavens did come,
Proclaiming a lesson mostly hard won.

"There is nothing safer than trusting God,
Anything less is a faith quite odd."

Parable Four: Trust

"Where have you taken me?" asked a flea.
"These bones are as many as fish in the sea!"

"I've come to join pachyderms, every one.
It's where we all go when life is done."

"Why on dry land?" puzzled a minnow.
"Out of water too long, you'll have a widow!"

"It's where whales swim one last journey.
It's how we depart for eternity."

"But what about me!" demanded the flea.
"Not for this fellow," implored the minnow.

Then a kind voice heard far and near:
"It's not too late. Don't shed a tear.

Trust in God and no other,
Then your soul in heaven will recover."

Parable Five: Sacrifice Explained

Why would an elephant die for a flea?
Isn't a flea more than a pain in his knee?

Why would a whale die for a minnow?
Isn't a minnow only around him for opportunity's window?

To answer this nonsensical ponder,
We must let our minds backward wander.

God became man and died on a cross,
His life for man's He considered no loss,

So an elephant and whale's selfsame sacrifice,
Makes more sense than why for man God gave His son, Christ.

Parable Six: Blinded

There once was a curious flea,
Who explored below an elephant's knee.

To his delight, he found two toes—
Between them, life would have no woes.

Settled in darkness and out of the light,
Comfort and safety became his delight.

Blinded by dimness he could no longer see,
Though he had eyes as perfect as could be.

Light was dark, and dark was light.
Soon he no longer cared which was right.

One day he faced a terrible woe,
A river's water filled between each toe.

His soul drifted to where fleas fear and dread,
To a place flea powder is evenly spread.

Parable Seven: A Soul's Worth

One day a whale's heart began itching,
As though what once existed went missing.

He searched to his left, and then to his right,
Straining his eyes with all his might.

Myriads of minnows in schools did abound,
Yet his heart knew one was missing, and could not be found.

Leaving the safety of his wise father,
He risked the ocean's peril to search even further.

Finally, he found him almost at death's door,
A shark's entrée—that's what he had in store.

Once delivered from the terminal shark bite,
"Why save me?" asked the minnow, shaking in fright.

"Why not?" the whale humbly replied,
While they leisurely swam home, side by side.

When the loss of one is measured by the safety of many,
Then the battle for souls is lost by Satan, our arch enemy.

Parable Eight: Life's Blood

How can a flea jump so high?
Why does it seem to disappear into the sky?

A flea doesn't make its home
On submersible hides, or scales that roam,

Only in warmth and comfort it will thrive,
98.6 degree flesh is what keeps it alive.

Although an extended life it may live,
Between homes, that always give.

Without it in measured time,
Mother Nature claims, your mine!

Though this proverb may seem strange and odd,
It's from Creation, and simply tells of God,

When He said life is in the blood.
It is something even a pesky flea clearly understood.

Parable Nine: Beyond the Garden

There once were two whales that lived long ago,
They breathed air, yet swam in oceans of salty H2O.

Male and female, their lives were beyond belief,
They lived in a paradise protected by a sacred reef.

Their days were filled with a life carefree,
They were granted everything their hearts and eyes could see.

Bored, self-absorbed, they looked for something new,
For what they had no longer would do.

They looked to the right, to the left, above and below,
Then what caught their eyes? A seagull with a fish in tow.

"We want to fly like the birds up there!
We want to soar heavenward, without worry or care!"

They jumped and jumped, high out of the water,
But they always fell like rocks that could soar no further.

A voice from heaven soon was heard,
He commanded them to listen to His every word.

"Since what I provided for you wasn't enough,
Your life of ease will now become very tough.

You are banished from the reef of abundance and perfection,
You will now roam the oceans without its protection."

This is why whales are seen today,
Soaring skyward in a brilliant but awkward way.

Parable Ten: The Trouble with Honesty

There once was a flea who pondered openly,
His queries fell on the ears of others unabashedly.

He questioned honestly what others thought privately,
Never accepting traditions as they always had to be.

Finally, his family was forthrightly told
Their son must live elsewhere on their elephant, for being too bold.

He was kind, and compassionate, and persistent to ask,
But his probing questions brought his character to task.

Not by the downtrodden and other outcasts,
But by those of high places who wore hypocritical masks.

His fame and reputation spread all over the elephant.
There had been no flea before him who caused such an event.

The elders' power, they thought, was at risk.
They were no longer prepared to just say, "Tsk, tsk!"

So a tribunal was held on a special day,
Every flea was there to hear what all had to say.

Unbeknown to our flea and his parents,
Despotic hordes were paid in blood to declare false precedents.

So in the quiet roar of these accusations,
He was convicted to die to preserve the flea nation.

"There has never been one like him," all said without hesitation.

"What he said and did changed our lives."
A following arose that still survives

To this day. It is thought he was resurrected,
For through him they all feel closer connected.

Parable Eleven: Origins

One day a minnow was swimming merrily,
For now, his life was rosy and carefree.

His mind began to drift and wonder
About the world he was in. He began to ponder.

"Where did I come from, other than an egg?"
It soon became a question his soul began to beg.

"Surely there's more to life than eat, sleep, and swim.
What will happen to *me* when all that's left is tail, bone, and fin?"

He asked the wisest of all he knew, large and small,
But none could give a sure answer, whether short or tall.

He decided he was not just a fish at the end of the food chain,
Though small, even he was known by a special name.

He concluded there must be a God in heaven,
As life around him was beyond scientific leaven.

At that moment he heard a voice from high above and all around,
Praising him for understanding this proof profound.

It said, "Not only do you have a special name,
But I know the number of scales around your frame!"

Parable Twelve: Of No Importance

Once there were two minnows of no importance,
Just two small fish in a sea of no significance.

They didn't stand out,
Nothing about them would cause a shout.

Just two small fish among many,
At a market they wouldn't cost more than a penny!

They felt their lives were just ho-hum,
Who would want them around to get anything important done?

All their small friends said they were very foolish,
Because to be something great was their big wish.

"You're just two small fish like the rest of us.
You'll never have lives to cause anyone a fuss!"

One day, like many of their friends in the sea,
They found themselves confronting their worst enemy.

Up from the deep they were hauled,
While all about them their friends bawled.

On a dinner plate today, they will all soon land,
From a net pulled to the surface, held by a human hand.

Our two small fish with big dreams were quickly discarded,
Judged to be too small even for one meal, halfhearted.

A small boy eyed the catch of the day,
He saw how the two small fish had been thrown away.

PARABLE TWELVE: OF NO IMPORTANCE

He took them and the bread he had,
And settled down to lunch, feeling quite glad.

Then he noticed a grassy hill nearby,
Where sat so many people, they filled the horizon's sky.

Two men called to him. "Little boy, come near,
And bring your food, so precious and dear."

There was also a kind and compassionate wise man,
And everyone sought to hear his loving command.

He asked the small boy if he would share.
The boy's heart was touched by his gentle stare.

As he handed over his loaf and two small fish,
He, like the others, pondered what the man could do with one dish?

Then after the meal was blessed by the Son of God,
He told his disciples to do something quite odd.

The crowd was divided by fifties and numbered,
And the disciples began sharing the loaf and two small fish, unencumbered.

There was so much food that they all had enough,
Everyone there felt full and quite stuffed,

How did this happen? How could it be?
Two small fish and a loaf fed five thousand and more by the sea!

This story teaches one thing very plain.
God does not look to the popular and strong to share His name.

He prefers the weak with big dreams, who are thought to be outcasts,
For He gives them strong hearts to last and last.

Parable Thirteen: Pride

There once was a flea, quite unique,
He loved to dance, and had very quick feet.

One day he danced with such power and grace,
He sprang into the air, although his shoes were not laced.

Higher and higher, he happily jumped,
His heart was pounding, and his soul was pumped.

He seemed to fly so high he couldn't believe,
He saw horizons of elephant hairs, far beyond what he'd conceived.

He said to himself, "I must tell everyone.
This elephant is much bigger than when our village was begun."

He hopped and hollered for all to come,
He gathered them together, to every last one.

He said, "When I start jumping over and over again,
Gather in one spot beneath me so I can catch the wind."

The fleas were so proud, they said, "Look what we've done!
No flea has been so bold before. We're all number one!"

At that instant and not a second more
Something happened they'd never seen before.

Each flea suddenly spoke in a different language and tongue,
So the tower of fleas collapsed to the very last one.

Parable Thirteen: Pride

Since that day of pride and arrogance,
The fleas drifted far and wide, without hindrance.

That is why fleas come in all sizes and shapes,
And they can all jump high without getting a scrape.

Parable Fourteen: It's All About Me!

There once was a wee flea,
And between you and me,
His own body was all he could see.

He lived on an elephant's back,
And there was nothing he lacked,
Because all day he would record and stack
All his food in containers, red and black.

One day, a hungry flea of lesser means,
Having recently arrived on the neighborhood scene,
Petitioned for food through the selfish flea's back door screen.
He replied, "No!" and included words somewhat obscene.

Time passed, which could be an hour or a minute,
Because flea lives have very short limits.

Our rich flea became fatter,
While our poor flea filled his life with what matters.

Then suddenly a bird swooped down on the elephant's back,
To fill his stomach with nourishment from what he lacked.

He spotted the two fleas, side by side,
But it was the fatter one he eyed.

So in one arrow-like strike with his head and beak,
He gobbled the selfish one, in a quick, mean streak.

Parable Fourteen: It's All About Me!

The humble flea recovered from facing death,
And realized after taking a deep breath,

Selfishness has its own unique reward in fate,
When one doesn't share blessings from Heaven's gate.

Parable Fifteen: A Whale's Tale

Sam was a whale with a tail as large as a ship's sail,
And from childhood he was the brunt of many hurtful tales.

Time passed and he grew healthy, big and strong,
But he swam at a distance from the pod that was quite long.

One day on the open water a terrible storm arose.
The pod and Sam saw a boat that on the waves fell and rose.

Suddenly a man was thrown overboard into the raging sea,
And the pod and Sam ventured closer to see.

A race ensued by a dare to reach this man first,
He was drowning in water that would soon over-quench his thirst.

Sam was behind his pod until a miracle occurred.
They were making fun of him being last, and he heard every word.

Suddenly, with all his might
He launched ahead of the pod as if in flight.

When he strained every muscle his tail unfurled to its full size,
It was twice as large and propelled him like a water jet, to his surprise.

Sam gently swallowed the man and didn't chew,
Because he heard a voice telling him there was something else he had to do.

So Sam found dry land and swam to its sandy shore,
And spit the man out. After three days in his stomach he was becoming a bore.

PARABLE FIFTEEN: A WHALE'S TALE

Jonah was the man who had his life saved,
And God put him through this ordeal to make him behave.

And although we don't read of Sam with the abnormally large tail,
We know a whale was there to help Jonah escape the gale.

God has a plan for all of his creatures, large and small,
And sometimes it's difficult to understand them at all.

Then, when God is ready to reveal his will for us,
No matter how strange, it will suddenly make sense and we will cease our fuss.

Parable Sixteen: The Elephant Who Refused to Fight

Long ago, beyond life's happiness and tears,
There was an elephant born in captivity during the height of Roman years.

He was bred to fight in the arena, day and night, before soul-less human cheers,
And due to his breeding, he was larger and stronger, beyond that of his peers.

Game after game, through blood and gore, he emerged the victor tall.
Soon he was known worldwide, because to fight, his owner answered every call.

One day, midst fire and brawl, he gazed into the eyes of a condemned, dying man
Who was a Christian, nailed on a cross, for from society he had been banned.

Our champion elephant saw the spirit of God firmly within this man's eyes,
So he lowered his tusks and refused to fight beneath those darkened,
heathen skies.

And the spectators grew quiet as they noticed something different
from the day before,
That within a moment, a holiness spread from the sand of the
bloodied arena floor.

God's presence reached all that day as Satan was chased permanently away.
Spears were dropped, shields were discarded, and swords where thrown
down to stay.

Then, for some reason no one could explain,
Since it hadn't happened before in recorded history,
The gladiators and animals and spectators
Vacated Rome's arena, quietly and unceremoniously.

All because an elephant saw in a Christian's eyes God's spirit
In the center of Satan's pagan pageantry.

Parable Seventeen: The Flea Who Refused to Be

Come close my children and listen here,
I want to tell you an interesting story about a flea, you need to hear,

Once there was a flea, who didn't want to be,
Because he surveyed his world and didn't like what he had to see.

"I'm through. I'm finished," he said in anger.
"There's something wrong in my world as I am not its manager.

I don't like my daily job of working for crimson nourishment,
It's such a drag from eight to five, and I receive little family encouragement.

Where I live is a hairy, middle-class jungle.
I would live higher up on my dog's hip if I just had a larger dollar bundle.

And my wife and kids, they always loudly complain,
'We never do anything or go anywhere.' Their voices drive me insane."

But then just when he thought he could take it no more,
The dog on which he lived walked by the Galilee shore.

Hundreds, maybe a thousand humans had gathered together,
They prepared to listen to this teacher, regardless of the weather.

There were so many gathered near that the teacher climbed into a boat,
And he faced the crowd from the water to speak, no matter how remote.

Just a few minutes seemed to pass, but in truth it was an hour or more,
And all who listened left changed and happy, no longer wanting
to settle life's score.

Parable Seventeen: The Flea Who Refused to Be

The flea was also a different insect who realized a new truth,
It wasn't the world that needed transformation. It was him—and not
with vermouth.

If he wanted to be someone good on the outside, and be proud,
It was what he was on the inside that could no longer hide behind a dark cloud.

So he resolved to be the opposite of what he once was.
He went home immediately and apologized to all for his attitude, including an
uncle and cuz.
And his heart daily grew so large his kindness was the town buzz.

All because of one man who showed him how the outside didn't matter,
Even if you were a tiny flea, had six legs, and siphoned blood into your bladder.

Parable Eighteen: Why Whales Beach Themselves

A marvel, a curiosity, a mystery—
Why do whales beach themselves in pods of plenty?

Scientists say some do it because they're sick.
Others propose they were wounded by predators that were more than quick.

Then there's the belief they weren't careful of navigation,
While playing or hunting near coastlines of their habitation.

But the truth is not even the smartest men have a clue,
So they continue to study and watch what whales daily do.

I have given this aquatic mammal's behavior great thought,
And I have a theory that perhaps sounds crazy, which no one has caught.

Are not whales creatures great in size, but sensitive one and all?
Do they not breathe like humans at God's ingenious call?

They travel in pods, or better stated, bonded families,
Where there are parents and calves that live together, in a state of dependency.

Centuries have come and gone,
Where man has done something wrong.

He has hunted and killed whales, weak or strong,
Then takes them from their ocean home where they belong.

So could their self-sacrifice have a profound meaning
As not all are sick or injured who beach themselves, baffling scientific gleaning?

PARABLE EIGHTEEN: WHY WHALES BEACH THEMSELVES

Perhaps their deaths contain a symbolic gesture of nature's
transcendent consequence,
To end their archaic slaughter by man replacing it with
Christian benevolence.

I believe their martyrdom points to the cross, which man knows is the better way,
Where Jesus put man before himself, no matter what others say.

And in his death he demonstrated selflessness as his communiqué,
In a life of respect practiced toward human, animal, or marine life every day.

Perhaps the whale's deliberate self-depredation is a signal to man,
That they are willing to die on the shore by their terms and own hand.

As a ransom through their blood in death, repeated for all,
They are requesting man no longer answer the whale-harvest call.

By realizing they are God's extraordinary creation, just like man,
And they have feelings and families that man harms when he can.

Then could we not say that man has a duty
To respect all God's creation, and not consider it booty?

Parable Nineteen: One Touch Opened the Bully's Eyes

Once there was a brutish minnow,
Who was in spirit deeply shallow.

But due to his girth, stole the other minnow's aquatic turf.

One night our school and its bully became nervous,
Because there was a storm above the sea's surface.

Suddenly, to the minnow's surprise, they saw the bottom of
a man's foot, quite a size.

The bully swam closer to get a better look,
But he got too close, and that was all it took.

When his fin touched the bottom of the walker's foot,
His heart and soul severely shook.

For the rest of his life he was polite and kind,
He went out of his way to help others, no matter their bind.

He returned four-fold all the turf he had taken,
And he distributed all he owned to the poor and forsaken.

He became known as a defender of the widow and orphaned,
For he used his girth to redeem and defend the rights of their misfortune.

The minnow school was baffled to say the least,
But they all had better lives because of the former bully's spiritual feast.

Then, one day when all was right with the minnow's world,
A tragedy occurred that those above the surface selfishly hurled.

PARABLE NINETEEN: ONE TOUCH OPENED THE BULLY'S EYES

A net was thrown over them when the minnows weren't aware,
And all but their new protector were caught in this snare.

Our protector could have run away and saved himself,
Instead, he determined how to release them to continue life on their ocean shelf.

But in the process of setting them all free,
He gave his life to make sure their safety would fully be.

Which goes to show all sceptics and critics who deny Christ's power,
That even a small minnow, through Jesus, can have his finest hour.

Parable Twenty: The *Too* Syndrome

Before the dawn of the English explorer,
Before the time when Anglo Saxon boats knew but few African shores,

There lived a mighty female elephant,
And as the herd's queen, she was magnificent.

All bowed down to her when she passed,
Everyone said her beauty was unsurpassed.

But little did other elephants in her herd know,
The image she saw in the river while crossing with the herd in tow,

Was replete with symptoms of the *Too* Syndrome.
For in her eyes ugliness abounded in every part of her body known.

Her feet were too round and flat,
Her hips were too filled with fat.

Her ears were too large and flapped,
And her eyes were too small. Didn't everyone see that?

This self-depreciation knew no end,
For years her personal secret drove her round the bend.

Then one day her path crossed with Queen Panther sleek,
And this depressed her more as they drew close, jowl and cheek.

Then when she listed her private view of her physical critique,
Queen Panther was in awe and couldn't speak.

Parable Twenty: The Too Syndrome

She caught her breath and challenged the Elephant Queen's litany,
And told her that her thoughts were really quite silly.

"For you see my dear, mighty queen of forest and plain,
It's you I envy, for all shudder and cower at your name.

You rule no matter where you go,
While I hide and sneak beneath where the grasses thickly grow.

Yes, you are very large, but your internal beauty epitomizes who and what you are,
That has drawn fame to your name both near and far."

Conclusion: Not the End, but the Beginning

The four of us pray that these parables have been of spiritual encouragement,
And that this won't be the last time you hear from us, although
we aren't heaven sent.

But we enjoy relating God's message in practical words all can understand,
That they in turn will inspire you to be faithful to Him, and take your holy stand,

Against the Prince of Darkness who is eternally bent
To steal your soul at your weakest moment.

For he prowls around like a roaring lion seeking to devour,
And we pray this short book will help you be vigilant hour by hour.

www.ingramcontent.com/pod-product-compliance
Lightning Source LLC
Chambersburg PA
CBHW051050030426
42339CB00006B/282